COMPOSER SHOWCASE
HAL LEONARD
STUDENT PIANO LIBRARY

Jazz Sketches

ORIGINAL PIANO SOLOS IN VARIOUS JAZZ STYLES

BY BILL BOYD

CONTENTS

4   Home Fried Potatoes

6   Oh So Blue

8   Move It!

11   Sound Advice

14   Ragtime Blue

17   The Bass Man Walketh

20   Swingin' Easy

22   Perpetual Motion

ISBN 0-7935-6959-1

HAL•LEONARD®
CORPORATION

7777 W. BLUEMOUND RD. P.O. BOX 13819 MILWAUKEE, WI 53213

Visit Hal Leonard Online at
www.halleonard.com

JAZZ EIGHTH-NOTES

Generally, slow ballads, rock, ragtime, and pieces written in six-eight time are played with even eighth-notes, as in classical music. The following designation is often placed at the beginning of the music:

Uneven eighth notes are played for
Dixieland, swing and most other styles, even though the notes are written evenly.

Tie the first two notes of the triplet together. The resulting rhythm is the swing eighth-note feeling.

Count: 1   tri - plet   2   tri - plet   3   tri - plet   4

The triplet rhythm with the first two notes tied together may also be notated in the following manner.

Count: 1 tri - plet   2 tri - plet   3 tri - plet   4

The following designation is often placed at the beginning of the music:

As the tempo increases, swing eighth-notes are played more evenly.

JAZZ GRACE NOTES

There are two types of grace notes played in jazz compositions. Jazz grace notes are usually one half-step below the melody note.

TRADITIONAL GRACE

played before the main note, as in classical music.

LAZY GRACE NOTE:

played on the beat together with the main note and released immediately while continuing to sustain the main note.

The lazy grace note is usually played with a double-note pattern where the grace note is on the bottom.

PERFORMANCE NOTES

Home Fried Potatoes is light rock with a bass line typical of this style. Play the left hand *legato*. The "lazy grace note" should be applied to the right hand..

Modern blues-chord voicings appear in the left hand in **Oh So Blue**. Try both types of jazz grace notes.

The melody for **Move It!** contains several common rock blues patterns. As for the tempo... move it!

The sounds of extended chords are heard in **Sound Advice**. Listen for the major seventh, flatted and sharped ninths and augmented eleventh chords.

Ragtime Blue is a rag with an occasional blues feeling.

The Bass Man Walketh features the sort of "walking bass" line one often hears in blues-style music. The left hand should be played *legato*.

A bluesy melody is accompanied by contemporary chord voicings in **Swingin' Easy**.

The right hand part for **Perpetual Motion** is similar to an improvisation which might be played by a jazz musician. As the tempo increases, the eighth-notes are played more evenly.

The metronome marks which appear at the beginning of some compositions should serve as a guide. The performance tempo is left to the discretion of the player.

Home Fried Potatoes

By Bill Boyd

Moderately ♫ = ♫ (♩ = 110)

5

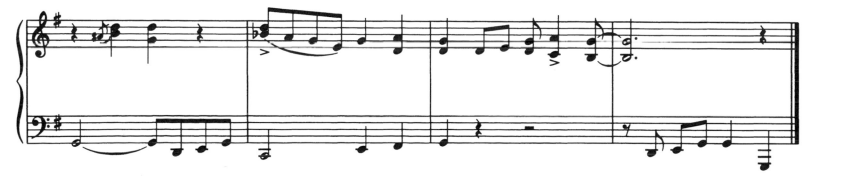

Oh So Blue

By Bill Boyd

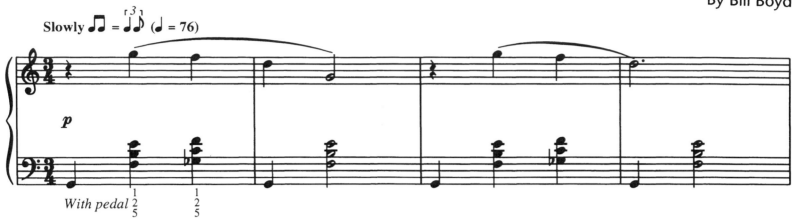

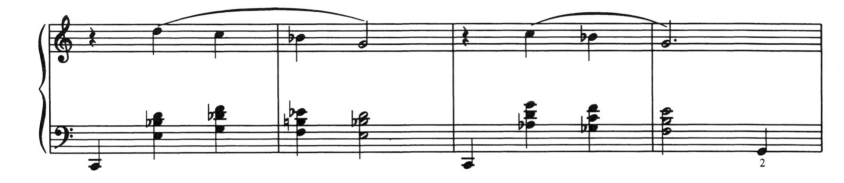

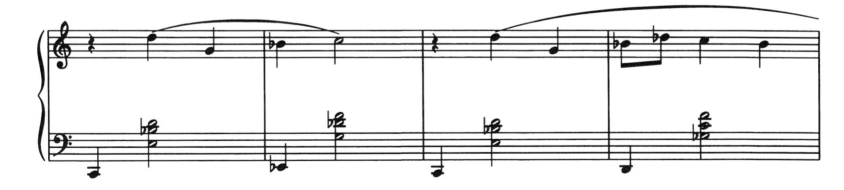

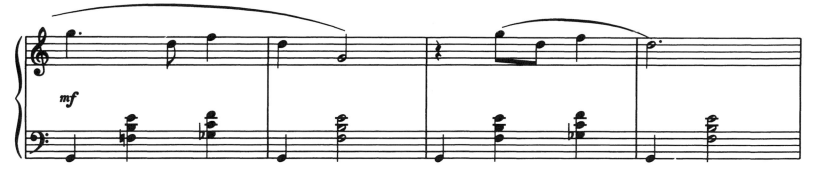

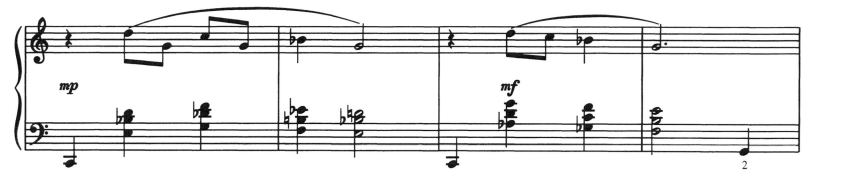

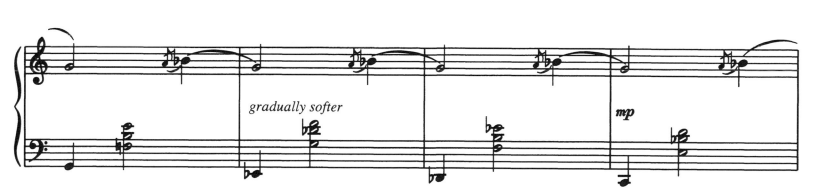

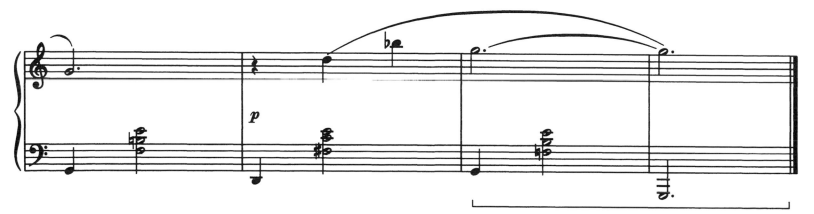

Move It!

By Bill Boyd

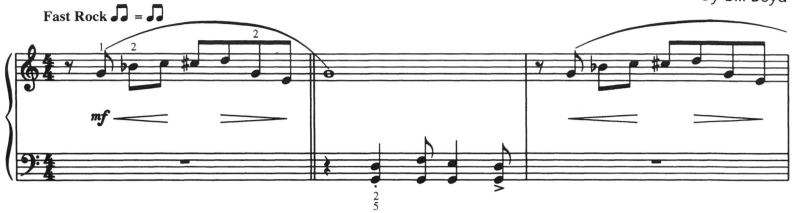

Sound Advice

By Bill Boyd

Moderately Slow ($\quarternote$ = 94)

With pedal

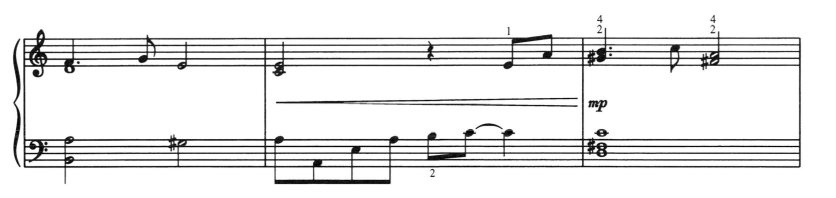

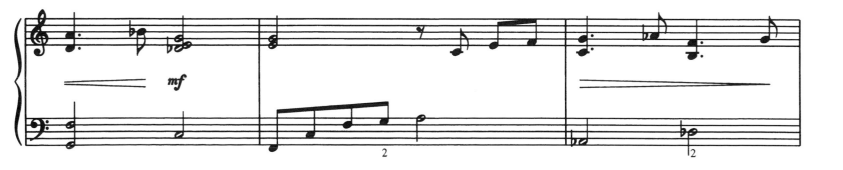

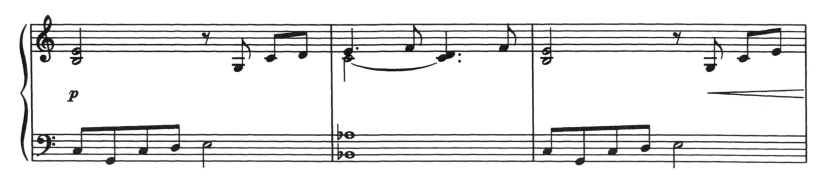

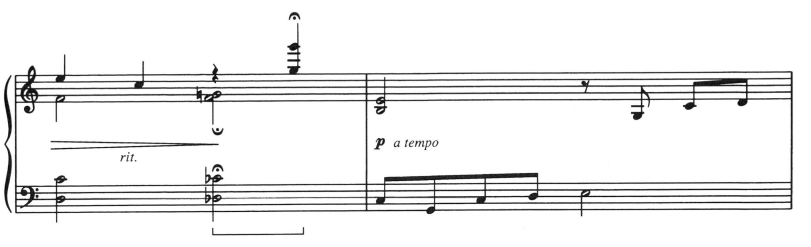

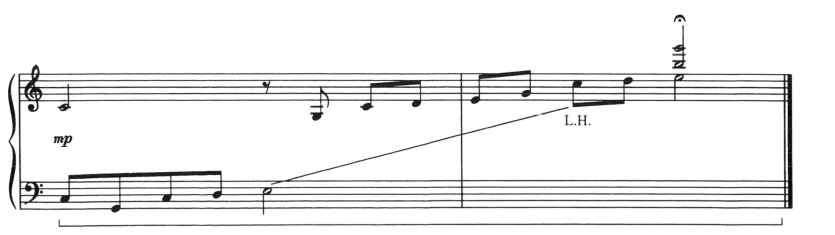

Ragtime Blue

By Bill Boyd

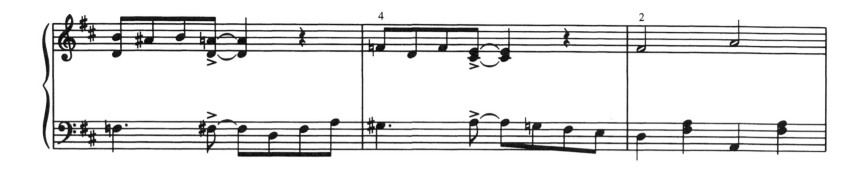

The Bass Man Walketh

By Bill Boyd

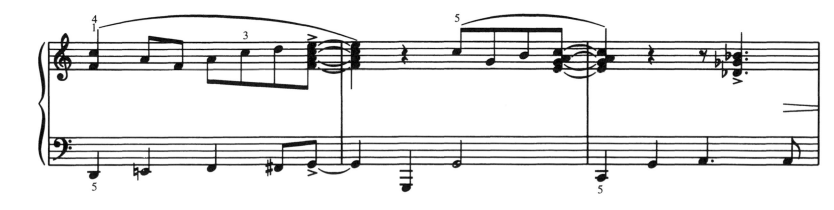

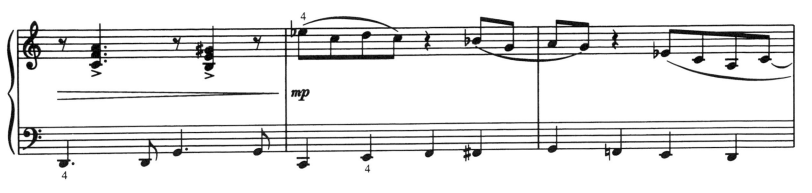

Swingin' Easy

By Bill Boyd

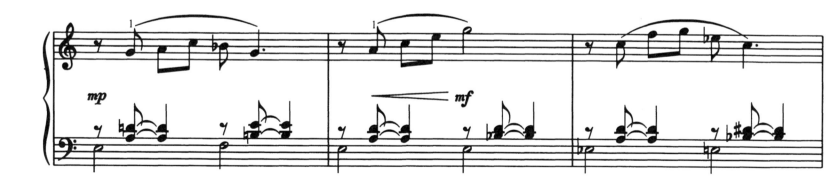

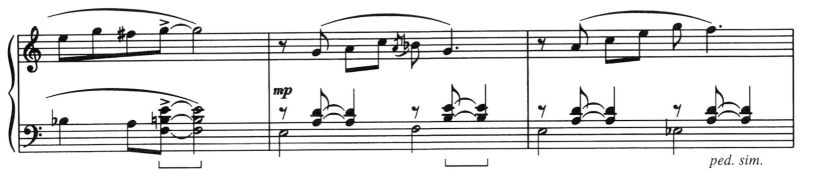

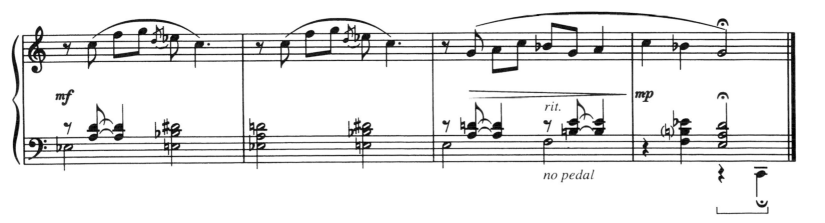

Perpetual Motion

By Bill Boyd

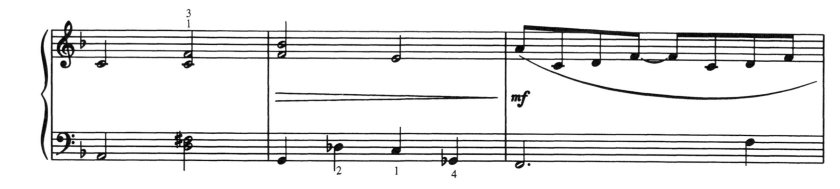

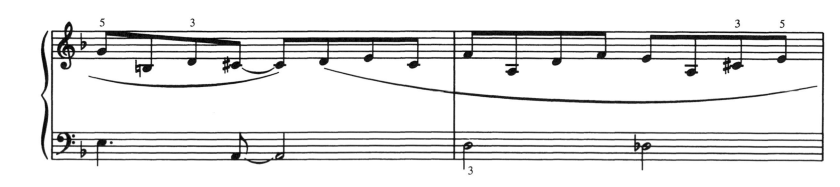

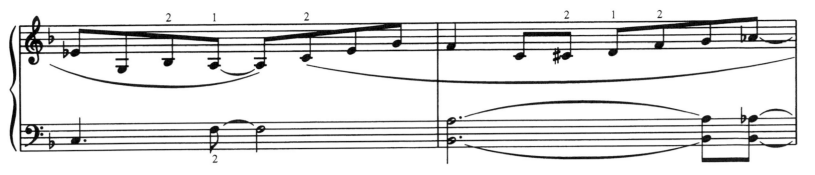

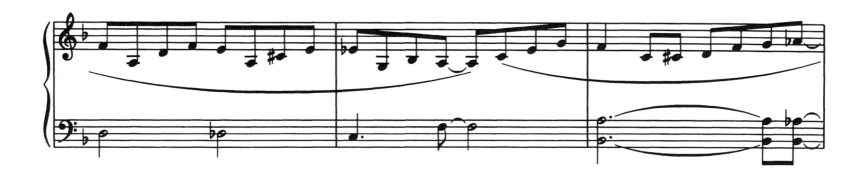

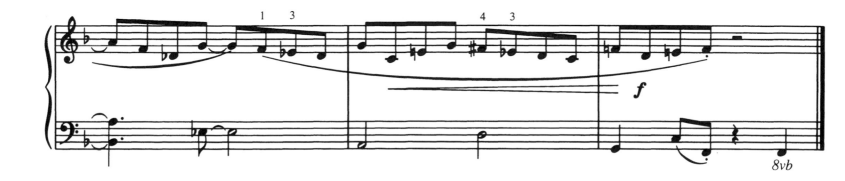

8vb